SUPER SIMPLE
EARTH INVESTIGATIONS

SUPER SIMPLE
MINERAL
PROJECTS

Science Activities for Future Mineralogists

JESSIE ALKIRE

CONSULTING EDITOR, DIANE CRAIG, M.A./READING SPECIALIST

Super Sandcastle

An Imprint of Abdo Publishing
abdopublishing.com

abdopublishing.com

Published by Abdo Publishing, a division of ABDO, PO Box 398166, Minneapolis, Minnesota 55439. Copyright © 2018 by Abdo Consulting Group, Inc. International copyrights reserved in all countries. No part of this book may be reproduced in any form without written permission from the publisher. Super SandCastle™ is a trademark and logo of Abdo Publishing.

Printed in the United States of America, North Mankato, Minnesota
102017
012018

THIS BOOK CONTAINS RECYCLED MATERIALS

Design: Kelly Doudna, Mighty Media, Inc.
Production: Mighty Media, Inc.
Editor: Liz Salzmann
Cover Photographs: Mighty Media, Inc.; Shutterstock
Interior Photographs: iStockphoto; Mighty Media, Inc.; Shutterstock; Wikimedia Commons

The following manufacturers/names appearing in this book are trademarks: Dawn®, Gedney®, Our Family®, Perrier®, Pyrex®, Sharpie®, Strathmore®, Westcott™

Publisher's Cataloging-in-Publication Data

Names: Alkire, Jessie, author.
Title: Super simple mineral projects: science activities for future mineralogists / by Jessie Alkire.
Other titles: Science activities for future mineralogists
Description: Minneapolis, Minnesota : Abdo Publishing, 2018. | Series: Super simple earth investigations
Identifiers: LCCN 2017946517 | ISBN 9781532112386 (lib.bdg.) | ISBN 9781614799801 (ebook)
Subjects: LCSH: Mineralogy--Juvenile literature. | Minerals--Juvenile literature. | Science--Experiments--Juvenile literature.
Classification: DDC 507.8--dc23
LC record available at https://lccn.loc.gov/2017946517

Super SandCastle™ books are created by a team of professional educators, reading specialists, and content developers around five essential components—phonemic awareness, phonics, vocabulary, text comprehension, and fluency—to assist young readers as they develop reading skills and strategies and increase their general knowledge. All books are written, reviewed, and leveled for guided reading and early reading intervention programs for use in shared, guided, and independent reading and writing activities to support a balanced approach to literacy instruction.

TO ADULT HELPERS

The projects in this title are fun and simple. There are just a few things to remember to keep kids safe. Some projects require the use of sharp or hot objects. Also, kids may be using messy materials such as glue or paint. Make sure they protect their clothes and work surfaces. Review the projects before starting, and be ready to assist when necessary.

KEY SYMBOLS

Watch for these warning symbols in this book. Here is what they mean.

HOT!
You will be working with something hot. Get help!

SHARP!
You will be working with a sharp object. Get help!

CONTENTS

WHAT IS A MINERAL?

A mineral is a natural, nonliving solid. Minerals are made of one or more elements. There are several thousand different minerals!

QUARTZ

Minerals have a crystal structure. Each mineral has its own properties, such as hardness and color. These properties help scientists identify minerals. They also affect how minerals are used in **industries**.

Minerals are all around! Salt is a mineral. So is the fluorite in your toothpaste.

SLATE

Some minerals, such as diamond and gold, are valuable. People mine for them.

Rocks are made of minerals. Some rocks have one mineral. Other rocks have many minerals.

CLEAVED FLUORITE

TYPES OF MINERALS

While there are thousands of minerals, most are rare. But some minerals are commonly found and used in manufacturing and other **industries**.

QUARTZ

Quartz is one of the most common minerals in Earth's crust. The clear crystals are often used in **jewelry**. Quartz is also used to make glass, paint, and electronics.

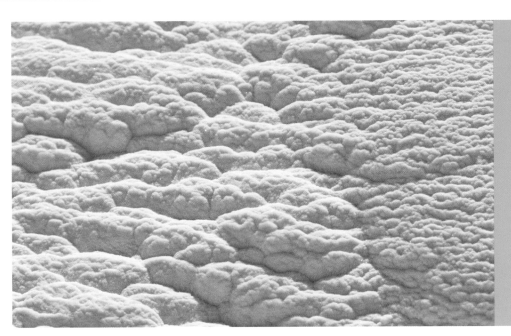

CALCITE

Calcite is the main mineral in limestone. Natural **chalk** is also made of calcite. Calcite is often used in construction materials such as cement.

HALITE

Halite is the mineral name for salt. Halite forms when seawater **evaporates**. Halite is used to add flavor to food, melt ice, and create certain chemicals.

HOW SCIENTISTS STUDY MINERALS

S ome scientists study minerals. They are called mineralogists.

Mineralogists study minerals in labs. They use microscopes to look at minerals up close. These scientists study the structure of the mineral. They check the mineral's hardness and color. This helps scientists identify and **classify** minerals.

Some mineralogists help mining companies. They explore an area to find out if there are valuable minerals there. Then, they find the best way to remove these minerals. Mineralogists also help invent new uses for minerals.

MICROSCOPE

FRIEDRICH MOHS

Friedrich Mohs was born in Germany in 1773. He was a mineralogist. Mohs invented a way to organize minerals. It is called the Mohs hardness scale. He put ten common minerals in order of hardness. He numbered them from one to ten, with ten being the hardest. Scientists use the scale to identify a mineral by its hardness.

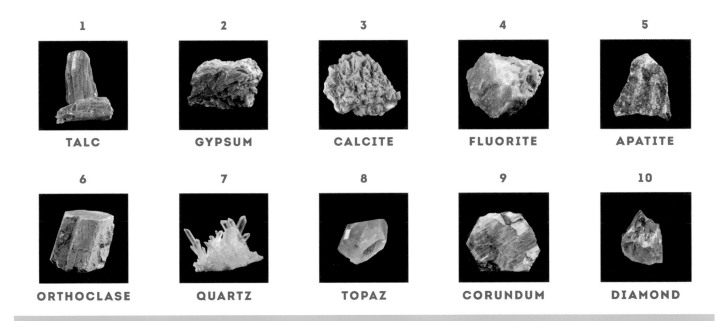

1	2	3	4	5
TALC	GYPSUM	CALCITE	FLUORITE	APATITE

6	7	8	9	10
ORTHOCLASE	QUARTZ	TOPAZ	CORUNDUM	DIAMOND

MOHS HARDNESS SCALE

MATERIALS

Here are some of the materials that you will need for the projects in this book.

ALUMINUM PAN	ALUMINUM PIE PAN	CHALK	CLEAR BOTTLES	COLORED PENCILS	DISH SOAP
DISTILLED WATER	EYEDROPPER	FOOD COLORING	LABEL STICKERS	MAGNIFYING GLASS	MEASURING CUP

TIPS AND TECHNIQUES

MINERAL WATER

OVEN MITTS

PAINTBRUSH

PAPER TOWEL

PENNIES

PLASTIC CUP

PLASTIC WRAP

VINEGAR

WASHERS

WATERCOLOR PAPER

WATERCOLORS

WOODEN SKEWERS

There are many rock and mineral kits you can buy in stores or **online**. Many of these kits include mineralogy tools. You can use these tools to study rocks and minerals. You can also do tests, such as scratch and acid tests. These tests help identify the minerals!

SCRATCH & ACID TESTS

MATERIALS: rocks, nail, magnifying glass, notebook, pen, vinegar, eyedropper

Scientists test rocks to identify and **classify** the minerals in them. Two common tests are scratch tests and acid tests. Scratch tests help scientists find out the mineral's hardness. And some minerals **react** to acids such as vinegar. One of these is calcite. So, dripping vinegar on a rock can show whether there is calcite in the rock.

1 Scratch each rock with a nail.

2 Observe the marks left behind on the rocks. You may need to use a magnifying glass. If a rock is scratched, the nail is harder than the rock. If the nail left a silver mark on the rock, the rock is harder than the nail.

3 Use a notebook to record which rocks are harder than the nail and which aren't.

4 Scratch each rock with another rock. This will tell you which is harder. The harder rock will leave marks on the softer rock. Sort the rocks according to their hardness. Record the results.

5 Drip vinegar on each rock with an eyedropper. If bubbles form on a rock, the rock **contains** the mineral calcite. Record which rocks have calcite.

CONNECT-THE-DOT CRYSTAL

MATERIALS: watercolor paper, marker, ruler, watercolors, paintbrush, plastic cup, water, colored pencils

All minerals have a crystal structure. This is the way the mineral's elements are arranged. Each mineral has a different crystal structure.

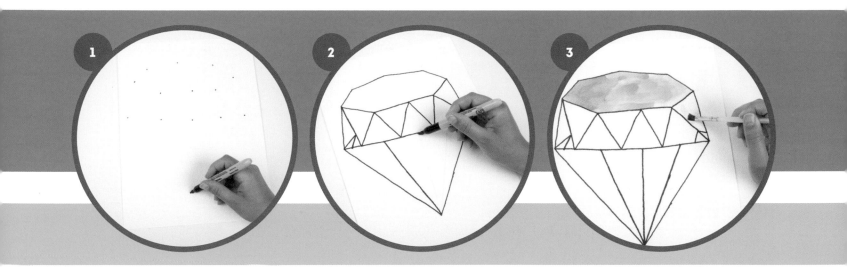

1 Make 15 to 20 dots on the top half of the watercolor paper. Make one dot on the bottom half of the paper.

2 Connect the dots to make your crystal structure. Use a ruler to draw straight lines.

3 Paint the crystal with watercolors. Let the paint dry.

4 Color the crystal with colored pencils. Create shaded areas on the watercolor.

HALITE CRYSTALS

MATERIALS: water, measuring cup, glass jar, oven mitts, salt, spoon, food coloring, ruler, notebook, pen, string, scissors, 2 washers, pencil, masking tape

You learned about the mineral halite on page 7. Now try growing your own halite crystals!

① Have an adult help you boil 2 cups of water.

② Pour the hot water into the jar. Handle the jar carefully! Wear oven mitts to protect your hands.

③ Add salt to the jar. Mix well. Keep adding salt and mixing until no more salt will **dissolve**.

④ Add two drops of food coloring to lightly color the water. Stir the food coloring in.

Continued on the next page.

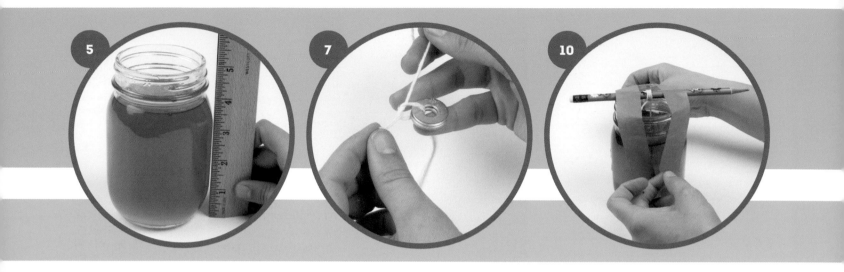

5 Measure the height of the jar. Write down the measurement so you don't forget it.

6 Cut a piece of string a few inches longer than the jar measurement.

7 Tie two washers to one end of the string.

8 Tie the other end of the string to the middle of a pencil. Make sure the distance between the washers and the pencil is less than the jar measurement.

9 Place the pencil across the top of the jar. The washers should hang down into the water.

10 Tape the pencil in place.

11 Set the jar in a cool place.

12 Observe the jar every few hours. Small crystals should start to form.

13 Leave the jar overnight.

14 Lift the pencil from the jar and observe the crystals.

15 For larger crystals, pour the salt water out of the jar. Repeat steps 1 through 4. Put the string back in the jar. Leave it overnight.

16 Repeat step 15 each day until the halite crystals are the size you want!

DIGGING DEEPER

Halite can be **dissolved** in oceans and salt lakes. Salt lakes often **evaporate** in dry seasons. Halite crystals remain on the shores.

Halite can also be found underground. Sometimes salt is pushed upward from underground. It forms a mound above ground. This is called a salt dome.

HALITE IN THE BED OF AN EVAPORATED LAKE

CHALK CHEMICAL WEATHERING

MATERIALS: 2 plastic cups, marker, vinegar, water, chalk

One type of chemical weathering is when the acid in water **reacts** with the minerals in rock. The reaction breaks the bonds holding rocks together. The rocks then break into smaller pieces. Pollution increases the acid in rain water. This is called acid rain. Acid rain can harm rocks, buildings, and other structures.

① Label one cup with a *V* for vinegar. Label the other cup with a *W* for water.

② Pour vinegar in the cup marked with a *V*.

③ Pour water in the cup marked with a *W*.

④ Add a piece of **chalk** to each cup.

⑤ Observe the cups for 30 minutes. What happened to the chalk?

DIGGING DEEPER

Some rocks, such as limestone and chalk, **contain** the mineral calcite. This makes them more likely to be harmed by chemical weathering.

Vinegar is an acid, like acid rain. So, the chalk you put in the cup of vinegar broke down more than the chalk in the cup of water.

UNWEATHERED (*LEFT*) AND WEATHERED (*RIGHT*) LIMESTONE

HARD WATER EXPERIMENT

MATERIALS: marker, 3 label stickers, 3 clear bottles, measuring cup, mineral water, distilled water, tap water, eyedropper, dish soap, wooden skewer, food coloring, timer, ruler, pencil, paper

Hard water is water that has a high mineral content. Soft water, such as distilled water, has a low mineral content. These types of water taste and behave differently because of minerals!

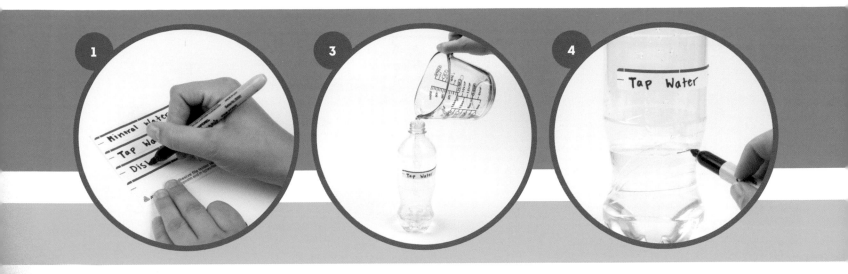

1 Write "Mineral Water" on one label. Write "Tap Water" on the second label. Write "Distilled Water" on the third label.

2 Stick a label to each water bottle.

3 Pour 1 cup of water in each bottle. Make sure the type of water matches the bottle's label.

4 Draw a straight line on each bottle at the top of the water level.

5 Use an eyedropper to put three drops of dish soap in one of the bottles.

Continued on the next page.

6 Mix the water and soap gently with a skewer. Try not to create any bubbles.

7 Add one drop of blue food coloring to the bottle.

8 Put the cap on the bottle.

9 Shake the bottle for 10 seconds.

10 Set the bottle down. Measure from the line to the top of the bubbles. Write down the measurement.

11 Repeat steps 5 through 10 with the other bottles. Make sure to shake them the same way.

12 Compare the bubble measurements for each type of water. Which created the most bubbles?

DIGGING DEEPER

Hard water **contains** many minerals. This is because the water comes in contact with rocks or soil.

Mineral water is hard water. Most tap water in the United States has minerals in it. So it is hard water. The minerals in hard water make dish soap less effective. It doesn't create as many bubbles.

Soft water has few or no minerals. Distilled water is soft water. Soft water doesn't change the effectiveness of dish soap. So, the bottle with soft water will have more bubbles than the ones with hard water.

MALACHITE PENNIES

MATERIALS: paper towel, non-metal bowl, pennies, measuring cup, measuring spoons, vinegar, salt, spoon, plastic wrap

Malachite is a common mineral. It is easy to recognize because of its bright green color! Oxygen in the air **reacts** with the copper in pennies. This creates malachite on the pennies. Vinegar helps the reaction happen faster.

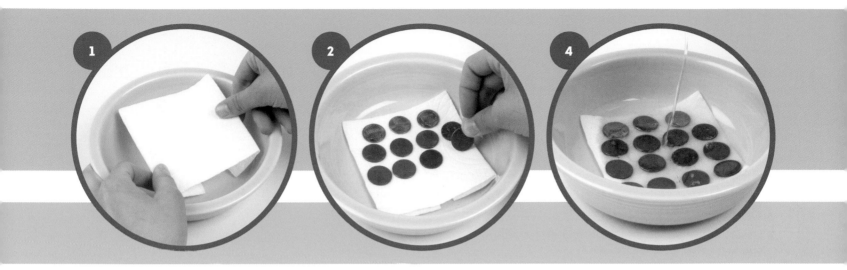

① Fold a paper towel to fit the bottom of the bowl. Place it in the bottom of the bowl.

② Place pennies on the paper towel. Pennies dated before 1982 have more copper in them, so they will work best.

③ Measure ½ cup of vinegar. Stir in 2 teaspoons of salt.

④ Pour the vinegar and salt mixture over the pennies. Make sure the paper towel is fully wet.

⑤ Cover the bowl with plastic wrap.

⑥ Let the pennies sit for a few days.

⑦ Observe how the pennies change over time. What color do they turn?

PANNING FOR GOLD

MATERIALS: paper plate, small rocks, gold paint, paintbrush, nail, small aluminum pie pan, large aluminum pan, water, sand

Gold is a valuable mineral. Sometimes gold is found in riverbeds. People use pans to sift through sand, dirt, and rocks to find gold.

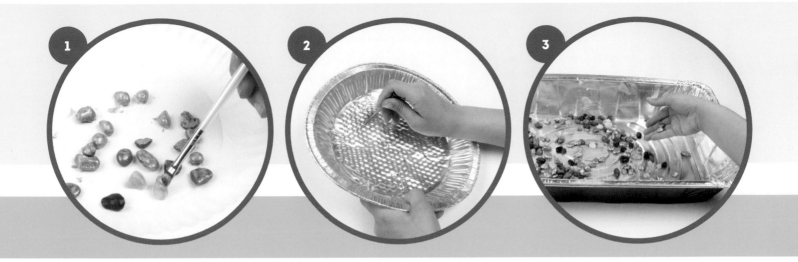

① Put some of the rocks on a paper plate. Paint them gold. Let the paint dry.

② Use a nail to poke several small holes in the small pie pan.

③ Put the painted and unpainted rocks in the large aluminum pan.

④ Fill the large pan halfway with water. Add sand so it's hard to see through the water.

⑤ Use your pie pan to pan for gold! Scoop sand, water, and rocks up with the pie pan. The sand and water should pour out through the holes, leaving just the rocks in the pie pan.

CONCLUSION

Minerals are important **substances**. They are all around us in water, dirt, and rocks! Mineralogists study and test minerals. They find new uses for minerals in our daily lives.

QUIZ

1. What type of structure do all minerals have?

2. Calcite is the mineral name for salt.
   TRUE OR FALSE?

3. What scale did Friedrich Mohs invent?

LEARN MORE ABOUT IT!

You can find out more about minerals at the library. Or you can ask an adult to help you **research** minerals **online**!

Answers: 1. Crystal 2. False 3. Mohs hardness scale

GLOSSARY

chalk – a type of soft, light-colored rock.

classify – to put things in groups according to their characteristics.

contain – to consist of or include.

dissolve – to become part of a liquid.

evaporate – to change from a liquid into a gas.

industry – a group of businesses that provide a certain product or service.

jewelry – pretty things, such as rings and necklaces, that you wear for decoration.

online – connected to the Internet.

react – to change when mixed with another chemical or substance. Such a change is a reaction.

research – to find out more about something.

substance – anything that takes up space, such as a solid object or a liquid.